To Ray, a true friend who brings light in the darkest of nights.

Seán Tobin

Night Poetry

AUSTIN MACAULEY PUBLISHERS™

LONDON ★ CAMBRIDGE ★ NEW YORK ★ SHARJAH

A CIP catalogue record for this title is available from the British Library.

ISBN 9781398448759 (Paperback)
ISBN 9781398448766 (ePub e-book)

www.austinmacauley.com

First Published 2022
Austin Macauley Publishers Ltd®
1 Canada Square
Canary Wharf
London
E14 5AA

Thanks to the many people who have accompanied me and enabled me to see more clearly. They have given more than they will ever realise. And also to Austin Macauley Publishes who have ventured into the unknown and helped share these words.

Night has a life of its own. We are creatures of the day. But night can be that time when our mind is most active, when our conscience can roam free in thoughts, imagination and dreams. Paradoxically, night maybe that time when ideas come to light. The day is full of 'busyness'. Work, family commitments, a social life to live. In the night hours, though, there is just the mind. "Just" the mind! As humanity, we plumb the depths of the ocean, we may launch ourselves into space, but can we know the mind? Our dreams are a conglomeration of the events of life. Of people we have encountered. There are instances in dreams we have no understanding of. However, they are there; real, alive, vivid. On waking, we may forget. Such is the power of dream and the power of the mind, though, that images can return briefly during the day. Inwardly we remember. Why? What do we need to hold on to and learn from? What is our mind, our dream telling us?

Night

Depths of darkness depending on what light.
Depths of darkness determining sight.
Darkness depending where night is lived
In city night, the depth of darkness depleted.

City lights beam down from on high,
Yellow hues, white light, invade our space as we lie,
On bed beneath duvet and sheet, secure behind curtain and blind,
Our sanctuary, our refuge from the daily grind.

City lights blot out countless stars of a universe so un-fathomable,
Vying with quarter, half or full moon so changeable.
The constancy of city's light guides traveller and reveller
Draws night-fly and moth, all creatures of night together.

Lying awake in city night,
Curtained window framed by invading light.
Still, spectral shapes of furniture, no feature seen,
Possessions of life, but in night what do they mean?

The urban sprawl of city life, sometime soon departs.
City lights left behind; deeper darkness starts!
In country night, senses inflame,
Life becomes wild, no longer tame.

Country night as city, time to rest, to leave the day behind,
Beneath duvet and sheet, behind curtain and blind.
In country night, black blanket adds its presence,
Windows not framed by light, but by night's essence.

No voice is heard, no car impedes night's slumber,
But in dark night, alone, no sense of what number
Of neighbours or friends close by?
Beneath black blanket of night we lie.

Alert to slightest sound,
Trying not to imagine what could be around!
A ghostly gathering of shapes, not spectral white
But black in the blackness of country night.

Here, nature supplies night's light show.
Outside the country retreat, no sodium light or LED, but night's sky is aglow,
And awash with bright stars of the universe, un-numbered, inspirational.
Moon and planets, to human eye so visible.

Nocturnal creatures, searching, screeching abound,
Hunt unknowing prey, snuffling, scurrying above ground,
Unseeing but all knowing. Night is their realm.
Depths of darkness their light, humanity no longer at the helm.

Night has a spirit of its own,
Life lives on in country, city and town.
Night workers live their day,
Night creatures own the sway.

For many, night lives in dreams
Where life is never what it seems.
For others, night lives too long.
A place of fear, to which, they wish not belong.

Night ends, dawn breaks through window, curtain and blind.
The life experienced, left behind.
Night's noise and dreams forgotten.
But night will return, unbidden!

Dark Night

Anxious, troubled night,
Mind, at full throttle, anxiety speeds headlong,
Even on coldest night, anxiety brings the heat of fright
Of all that is to come, inner voices throng.

They chant of failure that will come,
Of *"humiliation, weakness and shame"*.
On this night, the chant becomes an inward hum,
Heat brings sweat to the brow, inward trembles of self-blame.

The roar of anxiety's engine is constant,
But in the silence of night, crashing, mind shattering.
The roar, *"humiliation, weakness, shame"*. So blatant
In its assertion of what the future will be. Anxiety, all knowing.

This night, moonlit outside, is blackest of black.
The whitest of light cannot penetrate the darkest of this night.
Humiliation, weakness and shame, worthless. "It's self-esteem you lack!"
Self-esteem cannot be bought. Confidence would help to realise the light

That shines. But. In blackest of black night,
No light to guide, all that is to be known, *"humiliation, weakness and shame"*.
Anxiety – a machine, it creates fright,
Crushes, takes control of life, it steers the course. It is only me to blame.

This blackest of night continues, no dawn on the horizon,
No eight-hour period. The night of anxiety brings no rest.
"Conquer your fears!" is trumpeted in naivety. Anxiety will not allow, it lives
on
In dark night. *Humiliation, weakness and shame*, light fades in the west.

Journey

To rest, to sleep and slumber from daily toil of life.
Body aches, from work accomplished, another day complete.
Family fed, watered, entertained, work fulfilled now, a time to rest from strife.
A longing for sleep, deep, un-encumbered, replete.

Familiar sounds help to relax, this is home, the nest,
Nothing can disturb, nothing invades the space, chance to sleep.
Listen to breath that softens, tensions and worries, that all day have messed
With head and heart now disperse, before the leap, into the deep.

In the nest, into what should be a stillness of sleep, a force does invade.
The body at rest, the mind takes over!
Images, strange happenings perceived, cause movement of body that lies
In peace and comfort, events turn the tide, now senses alive, inner cries!

What does sleep awaken, to what world does it lead?
The invasion force of those from past and present, dead or alive
Are gathered as players in a pantomime parody, the stage, the head.
But it is not in the head, it is real, I'm there, aware of this other life.

Sleep is no longer restful, a journey into the un-known, destination, where?
On the journey, falling, lost, confused, shouting, screaming, screaming what?
Those once dead, resurrected by memories. Faces, once seen in love, now scare.
A cry to escape this somnambulistic stage of players. *"Get out! A player I'm
not!"*

In sleep, the conscience is awake. In sleep, time an instant.
A snapshot of life, the negatives, when exposed, are but a blurred picture.
Events of life, events of death, events of past when awake seem distant,
In sleep, the events so near, so real, so now, in sleep they have no allure.

13

"Catch the dream!" they say. *"Study it's significance as to the reality of life."*
The dream, a product of the night. It is my life; these players are mine.
"In my head they live, in my being they exist as I in them." Memories cut as a knife
Through what seems reality. Where does reality lie? In a timeless dream, in time?

Sleep Tight!

Night,
Black, no sight.
"Sleep tight!"
Dream.
Disturbed sight.
Fright.

Morning light,
Daily sights,
Slept too tight!
Dream lives on,
Disturbed sight,
Heaviness, night in day's light.

Sad

So many dislike dark, dreary evenings,
Affected by lack of light.
Nothing to do, nowhere to go
Gardens are out of bounds, out of sight.
To chill, no will, to venture out, feelings low.

Long evenings are but a distant memory,
When gardens hummed with activity.
Under a cloud of BBQ smoke,
The heavy aroma of scorched suppers pacify
The primal urge to inhabit the great outdoors that summer has awoke.

Dark evenings can give birth to creativity.
For in daylight dwells responsibility,
To work, to be 'out', doing something, going somewhere
Be busy, walk, run, garden, clean, visit. Why?
Because we can! It's what we do, without a care!

In dark of evening lies no responsibility to venture forth, so let the mind roam free.
In lit rooms, curtains closed against wintry damp and chill.
Fires and boilers pump out much-needed heat.
In comfort and security of home, create, roam with free will.
Follow where the mind leads, free from *"we should be"*. Retreat!

Many people will admit to being anxious about something; a forthcoming event, extra responsibility, work commitments etc. To be anxious about an individual thing is not necessarily an onset of long-term anxiety. To suffer in this way is a true burden. It hinders development. It blinds the person to their own gifts and talents. It curtails social interaction. It can crush life. Anxiety really does bring on the darkest of night. How then can a person move towards some semblance of light? How can they share the burden? There is, in some sense, a need to own anxiety. "It is part of me, of who I am. Does it make me any less a person?" Friendship and support helps to shine some much-needed light. Love and acceptance of another person enables the one with anxiety to share the burden. To be anxious occasionally is not always a bad thing. To live with continued anxiety is to live in darkness. Night is not only a part of the cycle of life. Its darkness can invade in the brightest of days.

Trapped

Trapped in a dream,
A ghostly scream
At faces in places, un-real, surreal.
Voices clamour to be heard, mine un-heard I feel.

Scream all the louder, shout for all your worth,
Someone's got to hear in this strange earth,
That those once known, now inhabit.
What is this place, where is it?

Am I awake? It must be real,
"Get me out of this ordeal!"
But nothing happens as the shout and scream,
Burst forth. *"Listen to me, this is not a dream!"*

Faces in places, they shouldn't be,
Goad and taunt, I'm unable to be free
Of the stress of this place,
Of the jumbled jungle, no space

To be myself! But this place is not un-real,
This place is my mind. In sleep, thoughts un-seal
`Themselves from boxes in which they are placed,
To live the ordered life; neat, tidy, memories erased.

But not in dreams. Now memories surface,
To create a production of little grace.
No clarity, or reality but bit part actors on a fragile stage,
Who come and go in a haze of sights and sounds and a timeless age.

Anxiety Dream

Daily tasks once undertaken,
Daily routine.
In the anxiety dream,
Become a mountain,
Unable now to climb.

"It's all going wrong!"
Fear, sweat,
Caught in spiral of descendancy,
Deeper, deeper,
Breathless, heart beats,
"What's going on?"

Why can't I do it?
Why do people look in horror?
In anxiety,
Deeper, deeper
Into the abyss.

Depression

This aspect of life can hit at any time, and for no apparent reason. It may have been deeply rooted for many years, then, suddenly burst forth upon an unsuspecting individual. As with anxiety, the word 'depression' can be misleading. We all get 'depressed' occasionally. Moods descend, but somehow lift at some point. To suffer from depression means the darkness does not lift, but, like a heavy fog, surrounds the sufferer to such an extent, the reality and beauty of life vanishes. Depression can also cause a person to realise life in a different way. To be able to see their life in the strangest of contexts. Little things become great. Analogies of one's own existence seen in the strangest of places. Sadly, as with many afflictions, we cannot lift ourselves from the darkness of depression. We need to be able to voice feelings, moods and emotions, to share all that is being felt. To share just what life is. Medical intervention helps. There is no shame in seeking that professional support. As with anxiety it can also help to 'own' the depression one may be living through. Feeling ashamed or feeling one is wasting another person's time can deepen the darkness. Seek support, value friendships, somehow accept feelings, live the depression and somehow, fogs begin to lift one day. They may descend on another day, but remember the light that began to glow.

What Do You Know?

"Don't worry, you're just depressed.
Get yourself up, get dressed.
You'll be better with some fresh air!
It's not as if they'll care!"

"But don't you understand? That's exactly what I can't do!
You've no idea. I feel like pooh.
(And not the bloody bear!)
I feel everyone's stare!

"I don't need you to tell me I'm just depressed, I know,
I live with it each day. The heaviness leaves me weak so
I'm unable to get dressed, to get so-called fresh air!
I don't give a toss. I don't bloody care!

"I don't want to look in the mirror, to wash and pamper
As though life's a ball. Just leave me alone, I'll only put a damper
On everything I know. No, this isn't just a bad day!
This is my life, I'm wired this way!

"Depression isn't a phase, fad or fashion,
It's alive in me, using the air I breathe, removes all passion
For the life once lived, when I felt free,
Lived life to the full, I could actually be me!

"Now who is me? Someone who has left life behind,
Or who life has left behind.
Keep taking the happy pill
It'll sort the moods, get you over the hill,

Of those days when you feel so heavy, almost wooden,
Wading through mud, sucking you down, you feel sodden.
You just feel, sod 'em all. Everyone can just p**s off.
Leave me alone, but in ignorance, they just scoff!

"No such thing as mental illness, pull yourself together!
Stop seeking attention, feeling sorry for yourself! Don't know how lucky you are!"
"Yeah right, at least I'm not ignorant of how others feel,
I know what life is. My world is real."

"I don't put on airs and graces,
I don't live an imaginary life, smiling faces,
When I feel crap, it's who I am,
Get used to it, to be honest I don't give a damn!"

Swings

Swing high, swing low,
What way will I go?
Life in perpetual motion,
Each morning having no notion
Of what each day will bring?
Is it light, is it dark, what is the thing,
That tips the balance to show?
Soon, I'll know.

Each day a different mood,
Be it bad, be it good?
Nothing specific kicks it off.
Will I accept or will I just scoff?
Current life seems alien somehow.
One day, frustration; *"For goodness sake! What now!"*
Another day, let it all slip by,
Why should I bother? Why should I try

To understand or argue the toss?
I'll live my life regardless, whose loss?
Not mine. Life is too precious.
Accept where I swing today, why be fractious?
No one else seems to worry
About all that goes on in this country.
Swing high, swing low.
"We reap what we sow."

Shave

Look in the mirror, what a sight!
Eyes hollow, rimmed by darkness where once was youth.
Those days when the chance to preen and pamper,
Might lead to making this a *good night!*

Now, a daily chore, respectable to look.
To wash and shave away the night, where looks didn't matter.
Looking in the mirror, now the daily round begins.
Wash and lather, scrape with razor blunting with each stroke.

Bristles float on a soap-scummed surface,
Tiny hairs once part of me, consigned to the swirl of unplugged basin.
These contain my DNA, ingredients of life, of my life, individual, me,
Washed away, expendable. In the mirror, now scrubbed face.

Look into the emptying sink,
What other parts of life, of me, of who I am have gone down the plughole?
Hopes and dreams, plans and schemes, once so important, never came to pass.
Who pulled the plug on all of that? Left me on the brink?

Just life, maybe, these were the excess.
Parts of life, expendable, it happens, dreams do not come true.
Holding a mirror up to life, we shave away empty ideas.
If they'd been fruitful, would life have been a greater success?

Windows

Looking through rain-streaked windows,
Tracing each drop from highest point to lowest.
En route, when water meets water
Each tiny trickle separates
To travel its own path,
Till at the bottom they converge.
One stream that flows down beyond the sill.
Drip. Gone.

Through rain-streaked windows
Views are distorted, no longer clear
As through obscured glass.
But the glass is clear, it is vision that is made different
By simple streaks of fallen rain.
Much-needed, often derided.
As rain eases, tiny drops adhere
To evaporate, then disappear.

Look through life,
Through mind's window,
To past experiences and people once-known.
Travelling from highest point to low.
Paths converged and separated, obscured,
One day to puddle in the pool of time,
Then stream beyond.
Drip. Gone.

The cycle of the seasons of life are the rhythm of our existence. Throughout the days of different seasons, we move from darkness to light, only to return to darkness… In the rhythm of the seasons, we see the emergence of life from cold dark ground. We see that life blossom and grow. We appreciate beauty, we witness its decay. We feel cold or chill, stifling summer heat. Rain, wind and snow. Crisp winter day, damp days. The spring greening of the land, the autumn browning of the trees. Each season can mark parts of our life, a life that moves between darkness and light. Life brings growth and beauty. It brings a difficulty of decay. The rhythm can sometimes be hard to accept, but the gentle rhythm continues.

Winter

Hard Days

Hard winter days,
Sun blinds, a cold haze.
Breath hangs on the air
Cold hits face, rosy cheeks bare.

Hard winter's day.
Once-soft earth, now as baked clay,
Hard, impossible to penetrate,
Crunches underfoot, can life proliferate?

Hard winter's day,
Sun's warmth cannot delay
The cold that seeps through layer upon layer
Of garments worn, now the betrayers.

Freezing frost and fog
Create a wall of cold, a duvet's highest tog
Could not deter from penetrating.
Numbing and debilitating.

Slow sun shines,
Slowly, slowly, touch of warmth, consign,
Frost and ice, to liquid, running down,
Hard winter has lost its pearlescent crown.

Soft Days

Soft winter days,
Murky mist hangs heavily and stays.
No wind, no breeze. Still.
Cloud. Grey invades city and field, with damp chill.

Soft winter days, once grassy parks and verges,
Muddy and puddled as green and brown merges
Creating the soft winter's tint,
Of khaki brown against grey flint.

No temperature fall,
In moist mild air, tall.
Spring plants surface from subterranean womb,
Premature. Through khaki brown, green shoots assume.

Exposed

Naked, bare, limbs stretched out.
Exposed to human sight.
Exposed to freezing frosty air.
Exposed to winds and rain, standing in fog-filled light.

Once I stood, clothed,
In colours oh-so-beautiful.
Shrouded in yellows, greens, crimsons, and gold.
I shimmered and glistened in warm winds and hot sun, bountiful.

I encompassed within me, life.
I stood proud and tall.
A symbol of strength and fortitude
Against the ravages of time.

Now look at me; skeletal, vulnerable, exposed.
Permanently rooted to this spot,
Aged by time in this arboreal abode
For as long as they let me live, or till I rot.

Tall Shadows

Sun hangs low, in a cloudless crystal blue sky,
Blinding the way forward, we move, unseeing.
Cold crisp air stings the face, eyes water in winter's cry.
Gloved hands deep in pockets, feet numb to feeling.

In low-hung sun, we move accompanied.
Tall shadows of the person we are, move before, move behind.
Distorted images, as in a hall of mirrors, tall, thin as a reed.
Life squashed into this black shadow aligned.

Shadows remain present on the journey,
present in clear light of day, in darkness and cloud.
Still they make their epiphany,
The shadows speak aloud.

Shadows of days long past, experiences lived.
Shadows of a darker side of life that obscure all vision.
Shadows seen in the winter of life, when days darkened.
Shadows to be exorcised with precise incision.

Life's shadows exist in crystal blue days, and days of grey,
Days when vision is clear and days when obscure
Days when eyes water, days when they smile at life's array.
Shadows of all shapes and sizes, when confronted can herald a cure.

Spring

Life erupts from its slumber beneath the black and heavy soil,
Where in darkness it lay dormant, in cold, wet winter.
As warming sun penetrates, nature begins its toil
Of growth. Earth's surface begins to splinter.

Fragile shoots spring, seeking sun's light.
Snowdrop, crocus, daffodil, tulip,
Ready to mature, to delight the sight
Of passers-by. After winter's bareness, nature will equip.

Once-cold muddy soil begins to green,
As grasses grow, as if nature has sown
New seed for the season to create the scene.
Colours to come, in bright array, in country, city and town. Mother Nature's
gown.

Above the earth, on trees large and small,
Buds appear to herald the coloured gown, a collection,
Of leaves that rustle, glint and glisten in the warming breeze before they fall.
Singing birds will perch, seeking spring's protection.

Summer

"Well, I think I can promise another lovely sunny day tomorrow!"
So speaks the grinning, groomed and gloom-free weather presenter,
An icon of meteorology, one of us it seems in their two-minute show,
A cheery smile, a wink, as though we're bosom buddies, as if they're the inventor
Of this weather to come, in order to please their audience, with summer heat.
Beach and BBQ feasts, in pub garden's beer-swilled gatherings we meet,
Or in gardens lounging, looking like raw, red meat, burnt fat,
A sweating mass of human-kind, in stifling sun, under an array of hats.

The presenter bears a mock-cheeky grin, as if offering gold,
To a waiting people in need of all that glisters. But is this offering beneficial?
"Oh to be 'continental', to be bronzed and beautiful, not pale and pasty as of old."
Café society is exciting, but here so artificial.
Solid summer sun beats down on houses designed for grey and mist,
When wet, windy, westerlies blow, bringing flint like cloud, penetrating mist.
Cocooned, we become, centrally heated, with thick carpet and curtain.
This is what we are used to, we're British, here evenings darken.

But not in summer months! Printed shorts, summer wardrobe,
Expose that pale, pasty flesh that soak up rays that's the British lobster effect.
Some, bronzed and body beautiful, creamed and oiled, proud to disrobe.
British summer, still and sultry. Humid air stifles, hanging as if a blanket
Draped over homes, no conditioned air to cool the stress of needed analgesic.
As windows and doors stay open, hot, heavy air carries sounds of TVs and music raucous.
A cacophony, shouting, crying, barking, the presenter didn't mention this!
Next time that painted grin is seen, they can keep their glorious summer bliss!

Autumn

Summer light and heat, move on
In the unending change of season.
Days darken, gentle autumn breeze pushes humid heat away.
Trees once shrouded in summer's hues of green,
Begin to change their cloak, as they sway.
Leaves turn golden brown, to provide an autumnal array.

Colours of golden brown, russet and red shimmer and glint
In weakened autumn sun. Colours with a tint
No human artist could create, now stand stately and tall
In this wondrous season of leaves that fall,
On damp soil or concrete of country, city and town.
Each landscape wears its golden crown.

Now leaves descend in stately splendour, kissing land in hushed silence.
Trees once clothed, slowly become naked in the suspense
Of the slow striptease, displaying the contours of each majestic body.
Now in nakedness they shiver in chill autumn winds, a parody
Of what they once were. The cycle of their lives,
Leaves that blossomed and adorned now gives

Life back to the land beneath which roots spread.
They descend to provide a fruitful carpet, soft as any featherbed.
From this rich carpet, will life flourish, compost for country or town,
Each leaf becomes one with soil, golden colours now muddy brown.
They provide the aroma of life, of earthiness, musty and damp, of autumn days,
When life starts to hide away, to shelter from winter's cold haze.

Mists

Fogs and mists rise and shroud the earth, giving an eerie blur to life.
Figures, once visible and clear, ethereal to the eye.
A world of unseeing. Sight obscured.
These are autumn days.

As mist and fog begin to thin
So soft, light enters in,
To transform the thick blanket of unseeing,
Into a curtain of sheer voile through which we view.

As light penetrates, a beauty is revealed,
Plants and trees glisten in watery sun.
On finest silk webs,
Iridescent pearls of light hang.

Each intricate web is decorated,
The spider's trap
Becomes a necklace encrusted and bejewelled,
Fit to adorn any monarch's regalia.

Mists ascend to remain,
Clinging to hilltops as if a cloak of silk
Draped to cover extremities laid bare,
Peaks, shrouded in mystery.

To Autumn Days

Walk through woods of trees in misty days, branches that hang low down.
Tall trees now skeletal, branch and twig.
Dew drops falling to carpets of golden brown,
Their pile thick underfoot, muffles sound of broken sprig.

Woodsmoke hangs upon the air
Its scent, a harbinger of comfort and cheer.
Where gathered around the hearth, ensconced in chair,
Warm from damp and chill, a glass of hoppy beer.

Conversations flow, as day darkens
Logs crackle and glow, sparks erupt,
And escape onto sooted hearth that blackens
With years of walker's rest, in hands their *'poison'* cupped.

The inn a place of refuge, over years,
For walker and local alike.
Refuge from elements and tears,
A place of friendship or solitary repose from life's hike.

Autumn days descend upon us all.
Summer days, long since passed.
No small wonder it's called the 'fall'.
As do we in life's long walk through misty days of the past.

Wasteland

Here, no haze of flower-covered grassy banks,
No birds in trees, chirruping their daily song.
No scene of pastoral idylls, no animals grazing lazily.
No smell of countryside, of damp earth or farmyard pong.
No picture postcard scenes of thatch upon cottage,
Surrounded by the English country garden. No beauty or rural realism.

Here the realism of an urban wasteland.
Hard, tarmac and concrete surfaces.
Here, tall buildings darken the street below, hiding sunlight.
Graffiti-covered walls in bright colours on drab backgrounds.
Wasteland dwellers determined to express frustration,
Tired of the blank backgrounds to their lives.

Here, scrubby banks, once grass, now an array of bottles and tins.
Contents consumed to fend off the realism of this wasteland.
Containers cast aside without a thought, or turned downward on railing spikes,
Resembling heads of executed prisoners.
Who are the prisoners of this wasteland? Who the executioner?
In these bushes, the implements of self-abuse lay.

With the bottles, tins and other paraphernalia of the 'high',
Lie the empty cups, of coffee once savoured.
The litter of the High Street coffee shop blights the land,
Blown in the wind, in ever-decreasing circles,
As are those who used them,
Blown around in the wasteland of their lives.

Through this urban land, trains come and go,
Through tunnels black, on into stations, going who knows where,
full of who knows who.
Their length penetrates, disgorging, engorging bored workers
Before it passes on its way, the once-mighty heavy metal sound
Fades in the gentle clickety-clack of train over points.

Here stand the monuments to commercialism past,
Empty edifices once shops, where once-consumers consumed
Emptying shelves of 'goods' once needed, the 'got to have'.
Satisfying the needs of the wastelanders.
Car parks once full, now devoid of life, save weed and grass
That pushed through cracked surfaces, laid to waste by changing times and
fashions.

On trains, in cars and buses, travellers move on to pastures new.
The dwellers of the city wasteland remain.
For this is home, where they belong.
They give to the wasteland, they take away, they abuse.
They give birth, they die.
The life of this wasteland lives on.

Four Elements

The four elements; Earth, Air, Water and Fire are the ingredients of life as we know it in the material and ethereal world. The elements conjure up many an image. Earth is our foundation. We grow and build on it and from it. It is the material. Air conjures an image of the spiritual; it is present but unseen. It is part of our being. Like the earth, water produces and sustains life in its many forms, and like air, is part of our being.

Fire is the element we fear in many ways. While it is an aid to producing food to eat, and protection from the cold winter days, as with water, fire can bring devastation in its wake. We are called to respect the elements of life, but do we? Do we simply take them for granted, even abuse them for our own means? The four elements speak to us, even cry for change and a greater realisation of their vital role in who we are as the human race...

Earth

I am called the feminine of the elements.
I am the fertile one, from me grow the nutrients
That they need for life. Plant and vegetation grow,
In me, they sow,
The seed for harvest, both small and great.
I nurture the seed, keep it warm, till time is right, while *they* wait.

I am called many things; the soil, the earth, the dirt, the land.
I am present, the material of life. On me stand,
The natural, and human-made.
I am exposed, or covered in concrete hard. I am the earth, on which are laid,
Necessities of life. I am foundation and bed.
On me, they build; from me, they are fed.

Do they respect the earth from which they survive?
Will my goodness forever be alive,
For them to over plant, grow and harvest?
Without a thought for my welfare, they abuse, and test
Me to my limits. Only so much to give,
I cannot continually thrive.

To 'feed' me, they chemically abuse,
Fertilise to encourage greater growth, so obtuse.
They rape and pillage for their own need,
With little thought for their disastrous deed.
I cannot give year after year, I am tired, old, unloved, ill.
One day, I will say, "No more". The earth is dead, you've had your fill.

Respect and fill me with natural goodness,
Leave me in peace, just for a while, please address,
The needs I have. I long to produce,
Be healthy, be abundant, but you must not seduce.
The pain, of machines that penetrate my being,
Leaves me un-fertile, but in arrogance you are unseeing.

As earth, I am your friend,
But what friend takes, takes, takes to the end?
Give a little back, feed me wholesome, enrich,
And I will give back, that which,
You long for and need.
Working as one, we can both feed.

Air

Air, un-seen, ethereal,
Air we breathe, for our survival.
Air comprised of gasses and vapour,
Air, nature's gift, inhale, pure.

Air, so fresh and clean,
Air to enliven, energise the human machine.
Air to clear heart and mind,
Air, so natural, so kind.

Air, fetid and stale,
Air, noxious, who'd want to inhale?
Air, polluted from belching gasses,
Air, hangs heavy over the masses.

"Clean the air!" environmentalists cry,
Clean the air, strip the skies
Of all that humanity inflicts,
Of all that humanity throws into the mix.

Air so fresh is what we desire,
Yet still we desire, plane, train and car fumes spire
Into the sky, what can we do?
Live with consequences or live anew?

Water

This planet of theirs is made up of me,
I am water, present in river, lake, ocean and sea.
In mighty ice caps, I am frozen, a wonder to behold.
In snow-bound landscapes, inhospitable, cold.
On salt water, with giant ships, they pleasure and ply their trade,
Cutting through my surface in both calm and storm-tossed tempest, as a blade.

From moist cloud, I descend to earth in drops of rain
To nourish their land, water crops on field and plain.
To replenish river and stream, great lakes alike.
I am their source of life, without Me, they suffer, fear strikes.
In drought, Earth becomes barren and bare,
An ocean, but of desert dust and dry air.

In me, life teems. Great whale and tiny fish survive.
Creatures both beautiful and ugly thrive.
Who can plummet the depths of great oceans, who can fathom,
The life that exists beyond human knowing, in sea cleft and chasm,
Sea bed, deep darkness dread to human kind,
Un-conquerable, un-habitable, no Atlantis will they find.

I am their great resource, I am their friend,
But yet, they show little friendship in return, the usual trend,
To rape and pillage, dredge and drag,
Unwanted fish, numerous in nets industrial, that sag.
Factory ships that trawl and delve the depths,
In-discriminate. The life of the sea it depletes.

Sea and river they pollute, discarded waste, un-wanted,
Poured into water, once pure, un-sullied.
Their waste lays waste to sea beast, fish and coral
Graceful garlands glistened, now bleached lifeless. Humanity immoral.
Bird and sea life solemnly united in death through plastic,
A convenience turned in-convenience so drastic.

Water increases as ice caps melt.
The consequences felt
Both far and wide. Sea levels grow.
Disasters show,
Humankind brings strife
To that which gives them life.

Learn we must from past mistakes,
Realise and do, just what it takes
To nurture waters, oceans and seas.
To value their life that the life may increase.
Water so valuable, so vital
To quench thirst and teem with life in its great array.

Fire

As fire, am I friend or foe?
They say they discovered me many years ago.
But I existed, long before,
My heat lies at their planet's core.
My heat and light guides their day as the sun.
I was present when their Earth begun.

Alive at earth's core, I have power
To melt iron and rock, which can fall as shower.
Thrusting up through mountains tall,
My power spews molten rock high, then to fall,
Covering landscapes, burning everything in sight.
Molten rock, my power, uncontrolled, My might!

They did not discover me,
But learnt to control me so I could not run free.
Controlled, I am their friend; controlled, I provide for needs.
When stable, they use me, to heat plants and meat so they can feed.
Once stable, they use me for light,
When the greatest of lights fades in their night.

Even as their friend, they use me to destroy and burn,
Innocents slaughtered, do they learn?
Why abuse my power? Why destroy all they have built?
Their control of me, un-natural and cruel, on them lies the guilt.
Anger and hatred, their fuel, desire borne of greed,
On one another's lives they also feed.

I am an element of life.
Yet out of control, I bring strife.
Will they learn respect for the natural world in all its might,
Not abuse what they are given? Do what is right!
As fire, present from so long ago,
I am both their friend and their foe.

Galicia, North West Spain. A proud people. "We are not Spanish! We are Gallego!" Proud then, not to be Spanish. A place of lush green hills and long beaches, a place of pilgrimage for many to "walk the way".

A place of rurality and peasant-like dwellings. Donkey and cart loaded with hay, belching tractors bring home the harvest. Like anywhere in Spain, a people who love to shout and make merry. Any excuse to party. Bars that come to life just as other places get ready to sleep. Cauldrons of 'pulpo' bubble away, Octopus and paprika, the Gallego delight!

A people who just accept loud music, whenever and wherever.

In tiny hamlet and village, everyone knows everyone as if they share one home.

Mountain-side vineyards, lovingly tended to produce the harvest of grapes for wine. Cheeses strong and tangy.

In Galicia, the sights, sounds and smells are what make the land.

Sounds of Galicia

Each day, a song played out as nature
Hums its tune.
Creatures bellow, bark and bray
Herald another day as hot sun disperses morning mountain mist.

Birdsong varied.
Songs of many notes or one.
Cattle in fields accompany,
Bells chime around beefy necks.
Their bellow from deep within.
Dogs keep guard of stately cows barking loudly. At what!

Flies buzz busily by.
Bees hum in search of nectar.
Butterflies in silent dance.
Warm wind blows bringing trees to life, leaves rustle,
Shimmering their many colours.
Chickens cluck, cockerel crows.

Day progresses in humid heat.
Over distant mountains, thunder rumbles,
Sounding nature's percussion.
A welcome storm, too shy to come.
An eagle overhead cries a sorry note.
Ascending, ascending, ascending.

Darkness, the black wall of night,
Crickets on cue, play their tune.
An owl cries its eerie hoot.

In the bushes, a scurry of what?
Cows still bellow and chime, dogs bark.
The song of nature is always sung.

In the song of this land,
Humanity plays its part.
Right or wrong?
Aren't we part of nature too!
Does humanity's efforts interrupt
Sounds of the earth?

The notes we bring,
To the song of nature,
For some offend the senses,
Preferring silence mixed with birdsong and leaves that rustle.
Bees busy at their work.
Humanity at leisure.

Voices travel far and wide,
Carried on the balmy breathless breeze.
Women's voices in lively debate.
Men's fast and furious
Deep and guttural.

Humanity at work,
Belching tractors and trailers,
Loaded with wholesome harvest.
Strimmer and saw, far and near
Buzz stronger than the humming bee.
No bird song now, songs of another sort.

Deliveries of fish, fruit and bread,
Arrive to the honking horns of car
As if brass instruments join the song.
Children accompany,
Screams of delight and sadness.
Just another day.

Storm

Thunder grumbles and rumbles, peak to peak,
As though the mighty mountains speak.
Thunder cracks, the mountain in anger and discontent,
Nature alive, fury vent!
The mountain stately, tall and proud,
Peaks point heavenward, shrouded in Godly cloud.

Cleft and valley, obscured from view,
Descending mists, paint a greyish hue.
Valleys of vine, luscious and green,
Only cotton wool clouds, now to be seen.
The mountain, once predominant and strong,
Now in patchwork pieces, mighty mists throng.

The energy of air in bright flash, distant,
From heaven to earth in an instant.
A charge of power, brightest of light,
Grey hues, suddenly bright.
Warm winds wander, they fill the air,
Energy felt, the mountain gives a share,

Of storm and tempest, mists and rain.
The burden of heat, no more a strain.
Lumbering clouds, distant now near,
Great drops of water, pure and clear,
Beat upon thirsty soil the once-hard bed.
In the storm, mountain and plane, watered, fertile, fed.

Divine!

Vineyards cling to mountain steep land,
Terraced, worked by hand
To provide, rich, red, robust
Fruity nectar to the taste for which many lust.

Morning mists enshroud
As if some heavenly cloud
Adding divine infusion,
To vine's growth in mountainous seclusion.

Sun bursts forth, through clouds
Mists retreat, heat grows proud.
Sunlit energy to the vine,
Once more, evidence of the Divine!

Ruby-red jewels adorn the vine,
Plump and luscious, till the time
Each vine grower, ascends steep tracks,
Like mountain sheep, to fill baskets on backs.

Produce ready and waiting,
Months of nurturing.
Ripe for the picking.
Harvest happening!